Addie Slaughter
The Girl Who Met Geronimo

Withdrawn

JAN 1 9 2016
Northville District Library
212 W. Cady Street
Northville, MI 48167-1560

Copyright 2011, Susan L. Krueger

All rights reserved. No part of this book may be used or reproduced or
transmitted in any form or by any means, electronic or mechanical, including
photocopying, recording, or by any information storage or retrieval system
without written permission except in the case of brief quotations used in
critical articles and reviews. Requests for permissions should be addressed
to the publisher:

Linda F. Radke, President
Five Star Publications, Inc.
P.O. Box 6698
Chandler, AZ 85246-6698

www.AddieSlaughterBook.com

Library of Congress Cataloging-in-Publication Data

Krueger, Susan L.
  Addie Slaughter : the girl who met Geronimo / by Susan L. Krueger.
     p. cm.
  ISBN 978-1-58985-197-9
  eISBN 978-1-58985-048-4
1. Slaughter, Addie, 1872-1941--Juvenile literature. 2. Frontier and
pioneer life--Arizona--Juvenile literature. 3. Arizona--Biography--Juvenile
literature. 4. Geronimo, 1829-1909--Juvenile literature. I. Title.
  CT275.S5229K78 2011
  979.1'053092--dc22
  [B]
                                        2010046064

Electronic edition provided by
www.eStarPublish.com
the eDivision of Five Star Publications, Inc.

 eStarPublish.com

Cover Design: Linda Longmire
Page Design: Linda Longmire
Project Manager: Sue DeFabis

Addie Slaughter

The Girl
Who Met Geronimo

A Division of Five Star Publications, Inc.
Chandler, Arizona

Dedication

To Adeline Greene Parks

who did not want her mother's

stories to be forgotten.

Acknowledgements

My thanks to Dave who saved me from

every computer crisis, and to my writers group.

They expect me to keep writing, and so I do.

~Susan Krueger

Five Star Publications is grateful to

the Arizona Historical Advisory Commission

for its official designation of

Addie Slaughter: The Girl Who Met Geronimo

as an Arizona Centennial Legacy Project.

www.azcentennial.gov.

Addie Slaughter

THE GIRL WHO MET GERONIMO

SUSAN L. KRUEGER, ED.D

WITH

REBA WELLS GRANDRUD, PH.D

VIII

Chapter One

I didn't think I was coming to Arizona to die but I almost did—and I wasn't the only one. But I'm getting ahead of myself. I'll start at the beginning.

I'm Addie Slaughter, the daughter of John Horton Slaughter. Later, he became real famous, but to Willie and me, he was just our daddy.

It all started in Texas where my brother Willie and

Me, Addie Slaughter, taken at Fry's Studio in Tombstone.

I were born. It's no wonder my mother, Eliza Adeline, fell in love and married my daddy in 1871. Daddy was a man

1

people looked up to. He was a Confederate soldier in the Civil War, and a Texas Ranger. Besides that, he was oh so handsome.

After Papa went to Arizona to look for a ranch to buy, he sent for us. Mother, Willie, and I got on the stagecoach at San Antonio and headed west to Phoenix. Willie wasn't even a year old, so he doesn't remember the ride. I was five and I remember how hot and dusty it was and how the bumpy roads woke Willie up and he cried a lot.

When we got there, Papa was gone. He hadn't expected us to come so soon and he had business in California. The people who met the stagecoach weren't happy to see us like Papa would have been. They realized we weren't just tired out from the trip. Mother, Willie, and I were all sick with a terrible disease called smallpox. We had fever and chills and ached in every part of our bodies. Soon we were covered with red bumps that looked like pimples. They got bigger and bigger until they burst open and pus ran out.

So, instead of a happy homecoming with our Papa, we were taken to the Pest House, a place where they put all the sick people together so others wouldn't catch the disease. We were still there when Papa returned. That's where he found us. Well, that's where he found Willie and me. For as the days went by in the Pest House, Willie and I began to feel a little better. But it seemed that as we got better, Mother got worse. I was sitting in a rocker with Willie, listening to the crickets when she died. Most people think crickets make a cheerful sound. They make me remember the saddest day of my life.

Papa came back to Phoenix to the terrible news that Mother was dead and buried. He took me and Willie home to the little house he had found for us. It was a sad and lonely little house. Neighbors were so afraid of catching smallpox they wouldn't come to help us. Even the doctor didn't dare become infected and so he just left our medicine by the gate. But we had our brave Papa to take care of us. He mixed hot water and mashed up bran into a paste and smeared it on our red bumpy skin. It did make us feel better, although we still itched something fierce. Papa knew that if we scratched open the smallpox bumps, they would leave scars on our skin, so he made little cloth bags to tie on our hands. Mine were often soaked with tears. After a time, our bodies healed but our hearts were still broken. I didn't know it then, but better times were right around the corner.

Chapter Two

My poor papa had two little kids to raise all by himself and a herd of cattle on the trail from Texas. What was he to do? He left Willie and me with a family in Tucson and headed to New Mexico Territory to meet the herd. While he waited for the cowboys and cattle to arrive, he got reacquainted with the Amazon Howell family.

Viola Howell, before she met Papa.

Papa had met them the year before when they were driving

cattle through Holbrook, Arizona. Viola was their young daughter. She told me later that she must have looked a mess at seventeen, " ... riding sidesaddle ... hair all flying about." I don't know if she looked a mess or not, but I guess Papa must have

Our beautiful new mama.

looked better than she did, because after a year, she still remembered seeing him sitting on the porch of the hotel. See, I told you he was handsome.

Anyway, at this second meeting, they fell in love waiting for the cattle to arrive from Texas. Viola's mama had a fit! She said Papa was too old, he had two little kids to take care of, and he was a gambler. Besides, they didn't know him well enough. Well, it *was* true that Papa was thirty-seven and Viola only eighteen, and he did have

Willie and me, and he did like to gamble. But, he and Viola made up their minds and rode off and got married anyway. Luckily, Viola's daddy liked Papa. He liked him so much he not only trusted him to take care of his daughter, he trusted him to take care of his cattle. They put the Howell cattle and the Slaughter cattle together in one big herd. They also put the families together and the Howells came to Arizona, too.

Grandma and Grandpa Howell.

My mother's family in Texas wanted Willie and me to come and live with them, but then a funny thing happened. When we visited our daddy and Viola in Sulphur Springs on the way to Texas, Viola fell in love with us, too! She said, "I'm going to be their mother and they're going to call me Mama." And we did! This young, beautiful woman was our mama and now we had a big, happy family.

Amazon and Mary Ann Howell became Grandpa and

Grandma and their two sons more like our brothers than our

uncles. Stonewall Jackson Howell was older but Jimmie

was just my age. Now I had someone old enough to play

with.

Chapter Three

W hen I was six or so, Jimmie and I got to go along
with Papa and Mama on a trip to Texas to buy
cattle. I was afraid to get on the train because it
was so smoky and made a noise so loud you couldn't think.
I could see Jimmie was afraid, too, but he pretended to be
grown up. Papa held my hand and Mama found us seats by
the coal stove so we would be warm. After we had gone
a ways, I began to enjoy watching the scenery whiz by. I
didn't know anything could go so fast as that train. There
were lots of things to look at...deer, elk, and once in a while
a buffalo. Jimmie and I got to stay with our Texas relatives
while Papa bought the cattle, and then it was time to start
back to Arizona. We only came part way home on the train
because we got off at Deming, New Mexico, where Papa

bought a wagon. We loaded up our stuff and started off to catch up with the herd. It got colder and colder, and then it started to snow.

Mama wrapped Jimmie and me in a buffalo robe in the back of the wagon and she sat on the seat next to Papa. That robe smelled like the buffalo was still wearing its skin, but it was the warmest thing we had and it kept out the wet snow, too. Even so, we were shivering. A stagecoach came along and when the driver saw how cold we were, he begged Papa to send Mama and Jimmie and me on with him in the stagecoach to Fort Stanton. Mama just said, "A woman's place is with her husband," and so we kept on going through the storm. The weather finally broke and we made it home. Later, we heard that the stagecoach had been attacked by Indians and that nice driver and all the passengers killed. It still makes me shudder to think about it. We could have been on that stagecoach if Mama hadn't refused to leave Papa!

Mama was already afraid of life in the West and hearing about what happened to that stagecoach didn't help. Even though she was scared, Mama went everywhere with Papa: cattle drives, business trips, and to deliver meat to the San Carlos Indian Reservation where he had a contract. Papa said Mama could see an outlaw or Indian behind every bush and a grave in every prairie dog mound.

One night, when they had to camp along the trail, Mama said she could see three men lurking around. Papa knew he wasn't going to get any sleep as long as Mama was worried, so he got up out of his bedroll and kicked a cactus to prove it wasn't a bad man. Another time, when friendly Indians approached them begging for tobacco, Mama made Papa throw it at them rather than stop to give it to them. She even cried every time they had to cross a river or a stream. Poor Mama. Papa said to just give her time and she would toughen up.

Chapter Four

In 1883, when I was ten and Willie five, Papa decided to sell his cattle and move us to Oregon. It had always been his dream to have a ranch on the Snake River. We got on stagecoaches and later the train for a long trip through Colorado, to Salt Lake City, Utah. Now that I was older, trains didn't scare me at all. I loved to ride on them. Then in Salt Lake City, we got on a stagecoach and headed north to Boise City, Idaho. That part of the trip was another long, hot, bumpy ride of five days and four nights. At one of the stops, the station agent told Papa that there were some "tough characters hanging around" and if Papa had any money, he should turn it over to the driver for safekeeping. Of course, Papa had a great deal of money under his shirt in his money belt. He had enough money to buy a ranch! Papa swore at the man and told him he had no money with him, but if he did, he thought he could take care of it himself! Then when they were alone, Papa gave the money to Mama to hide under her clothes thinking that if they were robbed, he would be searched but maybe not a woman. Once again, Papa and Mama made the right choice in not trusting that man. They learned later that the station agent was working with the stagecoach robbers, and we would have lost our money and maybe even our lives if they had believed him.

Papa never got his ranch on the Snake River. In Boise City, he began to hemorrhage from his lungs. That means that when he coughed, he spit up blood. Papa had always had problems with asthma and tuberculosis, and it seemed the climate up north made it worse. We all came home and Papa and Mama found us a house in Tombstone. Now Papa began to look for a ranch in southern Arizona, and he found a beautiful one. It was in the San Bernardino Valley with lots of grass and water for the cattle.

Grandpa and Grandma Howell moved into one of the

This is Grandpa and Grandma's adobe house at the ranch.

adobe houses on the ranch to help the foreman. Adobe

bricks look something like other bricks, but they are made

out of mud and straw and you stack them up with more

mud. The walls are thick, so the house stays cool in the

summer and warm in the winter. Old Bat moved out to the

ranch to help out, too. He was a black man who used to be

a slave before the War Between the States. He came out

from Texas with Papa to help work the cattle. I don't know

his real name. Everyone just called him Old Bat. Papa,

Mama, Willie, Jimmie Howell, and I stayed in the house in

Tombstone so the three of us could go to school but we did

get to go out to the ranch in the summer.

Mama was about to have new worries. When we moved to Tombstone, it was a rough, tough town. It seemed like the cattle rustlers and outlaws thought they could do whatever they wanted. They were just about to meet John Slaughter.

Chapter Five

The townspeople asked Papa to run for sheriff of Cochise County. He did and, of course, he won. Papa wasn't very tall but when he looked you in the eye, you knew he meant what he said. One man said Papa was the "meanest good guy who ever lived". Although he was never mean to us, I think I know what that man meant. Papa hated murderers and train robbers, and such, and he wouldn't let them get away with it. He just wouldn't. If a cowboy rode in to Tombstone who looked like he would cause trouble, Papa would tell him, "Hit the road!" If outlaws robbed or killed someone, he would ride off after them, usually all by himself, and he wouldn't come home until he got them. Willie asked him one time how he got the bad men to give up and Papa said, "I just say real quiet,

'Lay down or be shot down'." Willie said the way Papa said it gave *him* the shivers!

Papa liked being sheriff but Mama was scared half to death. When Papa was gone, she would ask our neighbor to sleep in the hallway or get her brother Stonewall to come stay with us. She insisted we keep all the windows shut and locked and the shades drawn even in the hottest weather. Doing those things helped a little, but Mama was always "real nervous" until Papa came riding in.

Here is Papa ready to ride.

One day, Papa took off after the Jack Taylor Gang after they'd robbed the train and killed the engineer. It wasn't the first time they had robbed and killed, either. Papa formed a posse and chased them from town to town to town. He came home with one of his ear lobes shot away. Mama just about fainted when she saw that! Papa ran for sheriff for a second term and won again, but he wouldn't run for a third time. Mama told him she just didn't think she could stand it any longer.

Mama had another nervous scare while Papa was sheriff. It was 1887 and there was a terrible earthquake. All the adobe houses and buildings on the ranch collapsed, including the one Grandpa and Grandma Howell lived in. Grandpa would have died, but Old Bat was there and pulled him out just as the walls and ceiling were falling down! The rest of us were in Tombstone and safe, but it was still frightening to look at the piles of rubble and think that some of us could have been under them, squashed. Papa figured the buildings had been built with about 7,000 adobe bricks. When they stacked up the unbroken ones to start rebuilding, they could only find about 120 that were still in one piece. All the rest were smashed to bits. Mama just kept saying, "Thank God we are alive." We *were* lucky. Especially Grandpa. We heard that more than 50 people died in Mexico, just south of our ranch, when their houses fell down on them.

One time, Mama's nervousness actually could have gotten Papa killed. She had removed the bullets from Papa's gun because she didn't like having a loaded gun lying around. When he heard there'd been a murder in town, Papa grabbed his gun and took off after the outlaw with no bullets in his gun. He must have been pretty mad but when he got home, all he said to Mama was, "I *say*, Viola! I *say* ..." I told you Papa was never mean to us.

Chapter Six

Every year as soon as school was out, Mama, Jimmie, Willie, and I would move to the ranch for the summer. It was our most favorite time of all. After we had finished our chores, Jimmie and I would go out to the barn and put bridles on a couple of horses. We wouldn't even put saddles on them. We just rode bareback. Mama would wrap some leftover biscuits or cornbread in a clean napkin and stick it in my apron pocket, in case we got hungry. Then she would kiss us and tell us not to get into any trouble and to watch out for the wild bulls. Every day she would say that as we rode away.

The ranch was so big we could explore and explore and never run out of things to do. We liked to go to one of the creeks or springs that were all over on the ranch and

The pond at the ranch.

catch pollywogs and crawdads. Jimmie would take out his
fishing line and hook and set it out in a likely spot. If he
had thought to bring a bit of cheese, he would put that on
the hook. Otherwise, we would turn over rocks until we
found a good bug to use for bait. Jimmie was always proud
if he could bring home a fish for dinner.

Sometimes we'd find a rattlesnake nest, and Jimmie and
I would spend hours throwing rocks at them. You know,
you can't get too close to the nest or you'll be sorry. The
babies are just as poisonous as the big ones, so you have to

watch that there isn't one under a ledge where you can't see it. We never told Mama that we were messing around with rattlesnakes or she might have put a stop to our adventuring. We *were* careful though and never

School days

got bitten. Now we know that it's better to just leave wild animals alone.

We also never told Mama about sneaking vegetables from Old Bat and Lavinia's garden. Old Bat was nice, but Lavinia was cross and cranky. She even chased one of our Mormon neighbor ladies out of the garden by waving a big knife at her! Can you believe it? And the woman even had the right to pick some things! That's what made it fun though. We would try to sneak a carrot or two or maybe a

22

watermelon when Lavinia wasn't looking and then get out of there before she could catch us.

We spent a good bit of time looking for arrowheads and old bones, too. Jimmie had a big collection of those. I liked pretty rocks and always had my eye out for something to add to my own collection. Sometimes we would bring home birds' eggs or a baby rabbit or a horned toad. Mama always said, "What did you drag home today?" like she was out of sorts about it, but really she couldn't wait to look at whatever it was we had found.

Mama had one rule I hated. She said I had to wear a sunbonnet, saying something about young ladies shouldn't get all brown and freckly. Once I thought I could fool her by taking off the sunbonnet and putting it back on just before we got home. When she took a look at the bow I'd tied, she knew what I had done and gave me a spanking. After that, I just pushed the sunbonnet back off my head when we were out of sight of the house and pulled it back up before we got home. Nobody cares if boys get freckles! What's it matter if girls do?

Chapter Seven

The evenings were fun at the ranch, too. Mama and I would take a ride after dinner. She said it was the prettiest time of day when the mountains turn a pinkish color and there is usually a cool breeze. When we got back from our ride, everyone would gather under the big tree and tell stories until bedtime.

Grandpa Howell loved to tell us about how he was the great-grandson of Daniel Boone. I could hardly believe it! Daniel Boone being such a famous explorer and all. We read about him in our schoolbooks, but Grandpa's stories were better. He told us how Daniel had escaped after being captured by Indians. And, how he had found a way through the mountains of Virginia to Kentucky so the settlers could move westward. They called it the Wilderness

Mama and Papa at the ranch.

Road because sometimes there weren't even any animal

trails. Daniel and his men had to hack their way through the

wilderness with axes. All this happened before we were the

United States of America and our country still belonged to

England. Grandpa was proud that his Great-grandpa Boone

had given him the name "Amazon." The Amazon I'd read

about was in Brazil and was the second longest river in the

world. That, however, is not the river Grandpa was named

after. He said Daniel named him for a river in Kentucky.

Sometimes people called Grandpa "Cap" and that was short

for "Captain" because he used to be a riverboat captain on the Missouri River. Grandpa told us great stories about that, too.

I liked it when Papa talked about the ranch and how he put his money down before he had even looked at it. Papa had been hoping to find a ranch ever since we got back from the trip to Oregon. Then he heard about this Mexican land grant that was for sale in the San Bernardino Valley. A land grant is when the government gives you land as a reward. Papa explained that when the Mexicans were breaking away from Spain, Ignacio Pérez was fighting with the rebels against Spain and later the Mexican government gave him this land grant. He built a hacienda which is a big Mexican ranch house. But the Apache Indians fought so hard to keep their land that the Pérez family finally gave up on the place.

No one had lived here for fifty years. When they left the ranch, they just turned the cattle loose and that's why there were so many wild bulls around. The Perez family sold the ranch to Papa for $1.25 an acre. No matter how often Papa tried to help me figure it out, I couldn't get my head around so much money. And our ranch was so big it wasn't even all in the United States! The border with Mexico cut right through the ranch and the biggest part was actually in Mexico.

Mama would get all dreamy-eyed when she talked about seeing the ranch for the first time. She said, "here was the valley stretching far out before us down into Mexico, rimmed and bounded by mountains all around ... the thrill of knowing it was all ours, that our future lay within it ... it was beautiful."

Chapter Eight

When Papa was no longer sheriff, Mama wanted to move out of the house in Tombstone and live at the ranch full time. Papa thought ranch life would be too hard for her and he wouldn't listen. Mama just puffed up and said, "Yes, Mr. Slaughter, we are moving to the ranch!" She knew that with cattle prices so low, Papa was worried he couldn't repay the money he had borrowed to buy the ranch. She said we "would put our shoulders to the wheel," meaning we would work really hard together so we wouldn't lose the ranch. Everyone did help, and things got better.

Mama and Papa loved children and sometimes Mama was sad she never had any babies of her own. She sure made up for it though! Lots of children found a home at

Mama and Patchy

the ranch. Sometimes, the families of the children were too

poor to take care of them, sometimes the parents were dead

or divorced. Mama gathered them in and made them feel

loved. She didn't care what color they were either.

One day Papa rode in with a big surprise. In his arms

Lola and Patchy were the best of friends.

was a baby. He had been riding with American soldiers who were chasing Apache cattle raiders. As the soldiers got ready to burn the abandoned brush shelters called wickiups, Papa poked at some bedding with his gun. The bedding moved and Papa realized he had found a baby. When they were unable to find the baby's mother, Papa decided to bring the little one home to Mama. The baby girl was about a year old and so cute with her big black eyes and shiny black hair that everyone fell in love with her. We started calling her "Apache May" because that was the month Papa found her, but it wasn't long before that got changed into "Pache," and then "Patchy." She was such a happy, smiley little thing, she became the pet of the family. Another girl Mama and Papa had taken in when her family broke up was Lola Robles. She and Patchy loved to play together and were fast friends. They even ate and slept together.

Patchy in the pumpkins

When Patchy was about five, the very worst thing you can think of happened. She was running around in the yard with the other children when they started playing in the coals of a dying fire. She got too close and her long dress went up in flames, and before they could be put out, Patchy was burned. Her lungs filled up with so much smoke that she couldn't be saved. It broke everyone's heart and we all cried and cried, especially Mama and Lola. Our darling little Patchy was gone.

Chapter Nine

L ots of famous people came to the ranch. You have probably heard of the most famous one - Geronimo. People said Geronimo was a chief and a medicine man of the Chiricahua Apaches. He was on the ranch lots of times, and if you don't believe me, just ask Grandma

The spoon Geronimo gave Grandma Howell.
Photo courtesy of the Arizona Historical Society Collections.

Howell. She will show you the hand-carved wooden spoon

he gave her. All of the ranchers lost cattle and horses to

Apache raiders, but some people said Papa didn't lose

nearly as many as other ranchers because the Indians had

a deep respect for him. It was probably true what they

said. That might explain, too, why Grandma was given the

wooden spoon and what happened to me later.

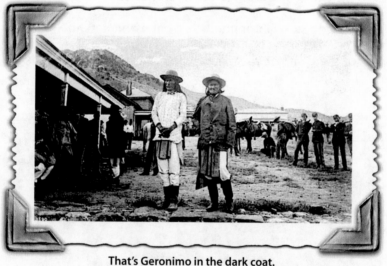

That's Geronimo in the dark coat.
(Digitally reproduced by the USC Digital Archive tcl2004,
California Historical Society TICOR/Pierce, CHS 3590)

General George Crook was also at the ranch. He'd

spent many years fighting the Indians but had now made up

his mind to end the war with the Apaches and settle them all on the San Carlos Indian Reservation in peace. He and his soldiers camped on ranch land by the San Bernardino Springs. Most of the soldiers stayed to protect the border but the general and a few men went down into Mexico to talk to Geronimo. The general must have been a good talker because Geronimo promised to bring his men up to the U.S. side of the ranch to surrender.

Mama was so excited that she and a friend rode out from Tombstone to watch, but it didn't happen. A terrible man gave the Apaches hard liquor and told them that they were all going to be killed when they laid down their weapons. So back to Mexico and into the San Madre Mountains they went, and General Crook got the blame. I don't think that was fair. It wasn't his fault at all. But that's what happened. Another general named Nelson Miles finally caught Geronimo and that was when I saw him.

I happened to be visiting the Olney family when they brought Geronimo to Bowie Station and put him on the train. We had heard that the army was sending him and

Photo courtesy of Addie Slaughter Greene

The necklace Geronimo gave me.

his band to Florida to get him as far away from Arizona as possible. There was a big, noisy crowd at the station because, of course, everyone wanted to see the famous Geronimo. There he stood, head held high, as proud as ever, looking at all the people who had come to see him. Could this be the blood-thirsty warrior I had heard so many stories about? Everyone around me was whispering and stretching to get a better look.

I was with the Olneys when he saw me. He motioned with his hand for me to come over and I looked around to see who he was motioning to. It couldn't be *me*. But it was. I couldn't move at first, but after a second or two and a little shove from Mr. Olney, I walked over and stood in front of him. I was shaking even though I knew he couldn't hurt me. This was Geronimo! He looked me right in the eye, took off one of his bead necklaces and very slowly held it out to me until I took it. And then, he did the most surprising thing of all. He bowed. To *me*. Just like I was someone important instead of a fourteen-year-old girl. All I could think of, was that he was bowing to the daughter of John Slaughter.

Chapter Ten

I was happy when I finished school in Tombstone as I wanted to see a bit more of the world. Mama and Papa found a school for me in Topeka, Kansas, a much bigger town than Tombstone. I

At school in Kansas.

was so excited to go! I begged that I was grown-up enough to go on the train alone, but Mama said no and went with me to get me "settled" as she liked to say. The school looked very fancy compared to the school in Tombstone.

I soon found out, however, that just because a building looks grand on the outside doesn't mean that it is a good place on the inside. Working long hours in the kitchen was bad enough, but I sure hated being hungry. How did the teachers think we could learn with our stomachs growling all the time? I didn't want to be a baby crying for my Mama and Papa but I just had to. I suffered for a while and then decided I wasn't as grown up as I'd thought. I wrote them a letter. Before it was time to get a letter back, they were at the school. The Head Mistress looked very pale and trembly after she and Papa came out of her office. She was still making excuses as we walked out the door.

My next experience with leaving the ranch to go to school was happier. My cousin Artie Slaughter was with me this time and we went to Field Seminary in Oakland, California. It was a wonderful time but it wasn't like it was easy. We studied for hours! We studied astronomy, literature, composition, and elocution, which is the art of public speaking. There were some easier subjects with less fancy names also, like handwriting. Remember when

I said I wanted to see a bit more of the world? Well, I began to realize I could "see" and even understand about the world through books, and I loved it.

Me in Oakland, California.

We called San Francisco, which is just on the other side of the bay from Oakland, "The City." Mrs. Hyde, our sweet headmistress, would announce that we were going to "The City" to see a Shakespeare play or an opera. We would get dressed up in our finest clothes and off we would go. Of course, we never went alone. We always had Mrs. Hyde or some of the teachers with us to act as chaperones. "Proper young ladies should always go out with a chaperone," Mrs. Hyde said many times. But it wasn't so much like they were watching us to keep us out of trouble, because the chaperones seemed to be having a wonderful time, too.

Those two years flew by very quickly and I was eager to learn even more. I asked if I could go on to college at Stanford, but Papa said he needed me at the ranch. I was disappointed but I also knew that Papa really did need me. He was no longer sheriff and as Mama had said before, we all had to put "our shoulders to the wheel" to make sure the ranch was successful.

Papa put me in charge of correspondence, writing letters to people about the ranch's business. I also did the recordkeeping, keeping track of everything we bought and sold so we could see if we were making any money. It was a big job and I was sorry that I never learned typing as I had to write all the letters in longhand. I had learned to write nicely, as that was something else Mrs. Hyde said proper young ladies should always do. Papa was proud of the letters I wrote for him and that meant the world to me. He kept me laughing, too. One day I was helping him with a letter and he couldn't remember the name of the man he wanted to write to. Papa said, "Put down Mr. Soda Cracker until I remember it." He remembered it later and I put in the man's correct name, but I always teased Papa that I was going to send the letter addressed to Mr. Soda Cracker anyway.

Mama always felt guilty that I wasn't able to go on to college as I'd wanted, so she asked Papa if I could go to St. Louis to study china painting. At first he didn't want to lose my help, but finally decided that since there was less correspondence and record-keeping in the winter, I could go then. This turned out to be another very happy time for me. I lived with the Mitchell family. They had come from Scotland and I had a terrible time understanding them at first, they talked so funny. My teacher was a chubby little German man who liked to tease me that he was falling in love with me. He always had a twinkle in his eye that let me know it was just a joke. It was hard to understand him, too, at first. They told me that I sounded like a cowboy with my western drawl! Can you imagine? They thought I talked funny, too. It wasn't long before we were all the best of friends. The Mitchell girls worked during the day, but at night we would go to an open-air skating rink. We would come home cold and hungry, and Mrs. Mitchell would have a pot of tea and a plate of cake ready for us. I loved being there, but by spring I was homesick for the ranch and ready to go home.

Chapter Eleven

Papa wasn't only glad to see me, but happy that I was there to catch up on the letter writing and record keeping. There was a huge pile of it on his desk for me to make sense of, as

Mama and me taken at a studio in St. Louis

Mama liked to say. It took me one whole day just to sort the papers and put them in the right piles before I could start to work on them. I pretended to be a little put out by all I had to do. In truth, it made me feel like a grown-up to know that I was needed and doing my part to make a go of the ranch.

The San Bernadino Valley is extra beautiful in the springtime, and lots of friends and relatives would come stay awhile to enjoy it with us. Mama also did her part to bring in some money by taking in boarders who would pay to stay at the ranch just as they would at a hotel. Some were important people who came for one reason or another. Two visitors in particular come to mind because they were so interesting in their own way.

One was a young man, a scientist called an ornithologist, who studied birds. He had been sent from The Smithsonian Institution in Washington, D.C., the biggest museum in the United States, just to study the birds around the ranch. We had lots of birds and while I liked to watch them, I never thought our birds were special until Mr. Condon began to tell us about them. Papa was always giving people nicknames and he called Mr. Condon "Hondoo." So that is what we all called him.

Hondoo had brought his guns and taxidermy equipment with him so he could shoot the birds and then stuff them so they still looked alive. When he finished stuffing them, he called them "specimens" and would carefully pack them up ready to take them back to be displayed in the museum. He needed a guide to take him out on his field trips every day at dawn. I knew every bit of the ranch from all the times Jimmie and I had gone riding so I was the best person to be his guide. Mama was still thinking that a young lady always needed a chaperone, but as everyone else was busy doing ranch work or house chores, she decided that I could take care of myself.

At first, I let Hondoo do all the shooting. But because he seemed to miss about as often as he hit, I began to think I'd be saddling up the horses at first light for weeks before he got all his specimens. So I began to help him out, so to speak. I *am* an expert shot. How could I not be, since I am John Slaughter's daughter? Anyway, things were going well and Hondoo was getting specimens of all the different types of birds when it happened. I guess it was both of our faults. Hondoo should have known not to get in front of the shooter...and I should have kept better track of where he was. I ended up shooting the hat right off of his head. I felt just terrible about it! I told him over and over how sorry I was. Papa made me explain why Hondoo had that hole through his hat and then gave me a serious talking to about being careful with firearms. Anyway, Hondoo decided he was happy with the number of specimens he had, packed up, and left soon after.

A Mormon by the name of Ammon Meshach Tenney moved two of his wives and their children to our ranch when having more than one wife was against the law in the United States. Papa had rented him a piece of farm land on the Mexican side and we would see him from time to time when he came to buy supplies from us. Their house was kind of funny as Mr. Tenney built it right on the border so that half was in the United States and half was in Mexico. That way, one woman was his American wife and one was his Mexican wife. One day he came to the ranch with three of his children. Because only me, my friend Cora, and

Mama were home for supper, Mama invited them to stay and eat with us. We had a great cook and Mama knew it would be a treat for them to have fancier food than they were used to getting. I set the table for seven and we were sitting down to eat when a bunch more children arrived to tell their father to come home for dinner. Mama could see them eyeing the food with big eyes and watering mouths so she asked them to stay, too. This was getting funny and Cora and I were sneaking looks at each other and trying not to laugh. Before I could get more plates and silverware, the last two of the children, a teenager leading a toddler, walked through the door. By now our big table was too full to squeeze everyone in. Mr. Tenney solved the problem when he said, "I'll just put the baby on my knee. I've been doin' this for twenty years." That did it! Cora and I burst out laughing and Mama sent us away from the table in disgrace. We had our dinner in the cowboy's dining room and kept right on giggling all evening.

Chapter Twelve

You might think that having coyotes howling outside your bedroom window at night or watching out for rattlesnakes would be the scariest things about living on the ranch. They weren't. The very scariest thing was when someone was sick or hurt and knowing how far it was to the nearest doctor. Because of that, Mama became a very good nurse. Remember I told you that right after she married Papa she cried every time they had to cross a creek and she shook when she imagined an outlaw behind every cactus? Papa said she would toughen up and she did. She *really* did. Mama treated Old Bat's abscessed ear, and cowboys with bloody gashes, malaria, and worse. Mama did all she knew how to do without a tear or a shake.

But sometimes, you just have to have a doctor. One

of those times was when Papa cut his finger badly and infection set in. Mama could see him getting worse with chills and fever so she put him in the buggy and started for Tombstone. When it got dark, they made a camp along the road. When Papa's breathing got more ragged and his fever even hotter, she bundled him up to keep him warm. Then my brave mama stood up in the buggy and whipped the horses to make them run through the dark the last sixteen miles into Tombstone. Sixteen miles! She couldn't see a thing but she knew that the horses had been on the road many times and they knew the way. The doctor took one look at Papa and said he was sorry but he would have to cut off the hand and part of the arm. He said that Papa could die from the infection as it had gotten into his blood and was spreading through his whole body. Papa looked him right in the eye and said "No! Never! I won't hear of it! Viola, take me home!" The doctor fixed the wound up the best he could and shook his head when they drove away. He knew Papa might die, but Papa knew he needed both hands to run the ranch. Papa also believed that Mama's tender care was the best medicine of all. Mama outdid herself with what she called her home remedies and, in the end, Papa and his hand were saved. The word spread that no one could beat Mama when it came to healing wounds and curing blood poisoning. Cowboys came from as far away as New Mexico to have her tend to their injuries.

Mama had lots of adventures along that road to find a doctor. When her cousin Jesse Fisher got kicked by a horse, his leg was broken and the bone was sticking out. When there was no doctor in Tombstone, she drove the wagon with Jesse in the back, all the way to the army hospital at Fort Huachuca. The roads were terribly rough and bumpy and, on the way home, the tired horse fell and broke a wheel on the wagon. What was Mama to do out in the middle of nowhere all by herself? She covered up the horse with a blanket to keep him warm and then walked all the way into the little town of Charleston for help. She was one tough lady!

One day when Jimmy was very sick, a cowboy rode forty-five miles all the way to Bisbee to bring back the new

Addie Slaughter Greene

doctor. He was a young man and I thought very handsome
and personable. He began to make frequent trips out to
the ranch whether anyone was sick or not. Pretty soon, it
became noted that he was making that long ride to spend
time with me. Willie and Jimmie teased me something

awful, but I didn't mind. I liked this man, Dr. William Arnold Greene, and was happy to say yes when he asked me to marry him. Papa and Mama liked him, too. Mama liked to joke that she was the happiest one of all that we would have a doctor in the family!

And so this part of my story is coming to an end. I have had more than my share of adventures as a child and young woman. Now I am going to be a doctor's wife in the small town of Douglas, which is not too far from the ranch. Another set of adventures is about to begin ... and I can't wait!

Read More About...

John Slaughter was an Arizona pioneer, a highly

successful rancher, and a sheriff who was able to tame

Cochise County. He
was also a politician
who represented the
county in the Territorial
legislature.

You might be
picturing in your mind
a man who impressed
people because he was
big and strong. In fact,
John Slaughter was a

John Slaughter

slight five feet seven inches tall. He impressed people, not with his size, but with his hard work, determination, iron-nerve, and his accuracy with a gun. He became a legend in his own time but hated to be pointed out or have people notice him. Once, when the family was attending the World's Fair in St. Louis, a man recognized John by the big hat he wore. John went immediately to the nearest hat store and bought a hat with a smaller brim.

John always said that he would not die in a gunfight but rather in his own bed. He did, at age eighty, on February 16, 1922.

Viola Howell Slaughter was a spoiled southern belle who didn't know how to cook or clean when she met and married John Slaughter. Through the years she transformed herself into a capable ranch wife, stepmother, nurse, and gracious hostess who oversaw a small empire. She was a superb horsewoman and, in fact, was about to set off on horseback with her brother Stonewall to jump the giant cracks in the earth left by the earthquake, when John found out and spoiled their fun.

Because Viola was nineteen years younger than John, she had many years of widowhood, which she spent in a comfortable home in Douglas, Arizona. She

Viola Howell Slaughter

found comfort in her grandchildren and the children of the many foster children she and John had raised. Only two years before her death on April 1, 1941, she rode her horse in the Douglas rodeo parade, still the fine horsewoman at almost eighty. Addie preceded her in death, dying suddenly of a heart attack just a month before the death of her dear mama, Viola.

The San Bernardino Ranch was the center of the lives of the Slaughter family for almost forty years. It was a huge property of over sixty-five thousand acres lying one- third in Cochise County in southeastern Arizona, and two-thirds in Sonora, Mexico. The lush grass and many springs and streams made it ideal for wildlife and later, cattle ranching. The area had been home to prehistoric people, Apache Indians, Spaniards, and Mexicans before John Slaughter bought the San Bernardino land grant. These earlier populations left behind stone tools, ruined pit houses, arrowheads, and crumbling adobe walls, making the ranch an exciting place for exploration, as Addie and Jimmie discovered.

The first adobe buildings on the San Bernardino Ranch collapsed in the earthquake of March 3, 1887. They were eventually replaced by many other buildings, and the large, rambling ranch house that seemed almost like a palace in those frontier times.

Geronimo's real name was Goyahkla which means "one who yawns." That name makes him sound sleepy and not at all like the fierce Apache warrior and powerful leader he was. Géronimo is Spanish for Jerome. Some people think that Mexican soldiers were calling to St. Jerome for help when the famous Apache and his band were attacking and the name stuck. It is strange to think that he may have been named by his greatest enemy, the Mexican soldiers. They had killed his entire family while he was on a trading trip.

While Geronimo is often thought of as a chief of the Apache tribe because he led other warriors in battle, he was really a medicine man. He was called a seer because he had visions of Usen, the Apache name for God. Geronimo's warriors believed that Usen protected Geronimo and gave him special powers. Some said he escaped from the soldiers time after time because when he walked, his feet left no tracks. Some said Geronimo's powers were so great that bullets could not enter his body. They were wrong about that as he was wounded many times but always survived. When Addie met him at Bowie Station she may have felt a little sorry for him as he was being sent so far away. It is true that he never saw his homeland again.   Like John Slaughter, Geronimo did not die in a gunfight. He passed away in bed on an Oklahoma Indian Reservation at the age of eighty.

The contents of this book are based on the research of Reba Wells Grandrud, Ph.D., historian for the John H. Slaughter Ranch, and on the writings of Addie's daughter, the late Adeline Greene Parks. Some dialogue and background have been fictionalized to enhance readability and interest. Photographs were taken from the Slaughter family albums and the collection of Dr. Grandrud, unless otherwise indicated. The author, Susan L. Krueger, Ed.D., is a retired teacher and reading specialist.

Curriculum Guide

Arizona became a state in 1912. What better time to share a book concerning Arizona history than at the time of its centennial. The setting of the story, the time and place, illustrates the Wild West heritage of the state. Arizona's Territorial Period was a time of struggle for all settlers and for the Native Americans. Some of the events are tragic and some are joyous. John H. Slaughter was a famous man, and in this story we learn about his family. While sharing this book with your child or in the classroom, follow the model of good reading instruction by choosing one or more pre-reading activities to focus thoughts on the story. Then, in order to foster comprehension, continue guiding the reading itself with reading strategies. After reading the story, follow up with post-reading activities to increase understanding.

Pre Reading Activities:

• **Preview vocabulary:** pest house, smallpox, foreman, rustler, posse, adobe, Chiricahua

• **Preview family names:** Addie Slaughter, Willie Slaughter, John Horton Slaughter, Eliza Adeline Slaughter, Amazon Howell, Mary Ann Howell, Jimmie Howell, Stonewall Jackson Howell, Viola Howell Slaughter.

• **Learn other characters:** Old Bat, Lavinia, Geronimo, Dr. William Arnold Greene.

• **Learn the relationship among the characters:** draw and label a family tree for the Slaughter family to learn their relationships.

The story begins in 1871. Can you imagine what the towns and houses looked like? Think about any cowboy movies of the Old West that you might have seen.

Use the internet and search for Cochise County history and John Slaughter to find his picture and clothing that men and women wore at the time. Also try searching Arizona history, 1880s; Sheriff John Slaughter, the San Bernardino Ranch, and the John H. Slaughter Ranch.

During Reading Activities

Use a map of the US and northern Mexico or draw your own. The Slaughter family and Addie traveled often. As Addie Slaughter moves from place to place, mark and label the travels on the map. Use Google Earth to find the Slaughter Ranch today.

Addie Slaughter is the narrator of this story. How old do you think she is when she is looking back and telling her life? Do you think that each section came from a diary or is she remembering it all at once?

Viola Slaughter is a complex character, too, and Addie tells many details about her. As you read, make a list of her personality traits.

The Slaughter family and others met many Native Americans and sometimes there were tragic events. How and why were the meetings with the Slaughter family members positive? Was there also a sad aspect to Addie's meeting with Geronimo?

Addie's narration glows with pride for her father. His behavior with his family is different from his behavior as sheriff. Compare his family life to his work using a T-chart.

(A T-Chart is used for listing two separate viewpoints of a topic. Topics can include anything that can be cleanly divided into two opposing views. For example, evaluating the pros and cons of a major decision is a common use of T-Charts. Other opposing views that work well include facts versus opinions, advantages versus disadvantages or strengths versus weaknesses.)

Family	Job

Post Reading Activities

Addie Slaughter had many adventures in her life. Create a character map that illustrates events in the story that affect her. Different samples can be found at www. ThinkPort.org - simply type in "character map" in the search box.

Why do you think Geronimo honored Addie?

Life was harsh in the late 1800s. Medical treatments and safety features that we have today were not available; even seeing a doctor was not quick nor easy. What are some sad events in the story that might not turn out so badly today?

The Slaughter family had pride in being educated. How is this shown in the book?

Further study:

- Crickets made Addie sad. Research the folklore of crickets and their use in other cultures.

- How was smallpox controlled and finally eliminated?

- Who were the Texas Rangers?

- Who was John H. Slaughter and what are some of his legends?

- Who was Geronimo and how did he evade capture?

- What were the main stagecoach routes through Arizona?

- Participate in National History Day projects through the Arizona Historical Society:

  http://www.arizonahistoricalsociety.org/nhd/default.asp

• Learn more about Arizona History through the Arizona Memory Project at the Arizona State Library, Archives and Records: http://www.lib.az.us/Default.aspx

• Find the Slaughter Ranch online: http://www.slaughterranch.com/slaughterranch/index.html

• Find brief oral histories of Cochise County, Arizona: www.mycochise.com/oralhist.php

About the Author

An Arizona-based
teacher for 32 years,
Susan L. Krueger, Ed.D.,
earned her undergraduate,
Master's and Doctorate
degrees from Northern
Arizona University. She
taught first-grade students
in Holbrook, elementary
and junior high remedial

Susan L. Krueger

readers in Flagstaff and elementary remedial readers in the
Cartwright District in Phoenix. She also taught adults at
Chapman University and Arizona State University West.

Though she officially "retired" in 2000, Krueger works

now as much as she ever has. She joined the Phoenix Art Museum docent program and is currently their research chair. In addition, Krueger gives many slide show talks on art-related topics around the Valley of the Sun. She also writes research papers on art objects for use by museum docents.

Krueger became interested in Addie Slaughter's story when her writers' group visited the Slaughter Ranch outside Douglas, Ariz. While there, Arizona Culturekeeper Dr. Reba Wells Grandrud, the John H. Slaughter Ranch historian, presented a slide show and discussed the adventures of the Slaughter family and the Slaughter Ranch. Krueger immediately realized what a wonderful children's book the information would make. After much research and hours of collaboration with Dr. Grandrud on the historical legacy of the Slaughters, Krueger wrote Addie Slaughter: The Girl Who Met Geronimo, which is being published by Five Star Publications.

Born in Northern Calif., Krueger now lives in Phoenix, Arizona.

About the Historian

Dr. Reba Wells
Grandrud, Ph.D., a
recipient of the 2010
Arizona Culture Keeper
Award, earned degrees
in education and history
from the University
of New Mexico,
before moving from

Dr. Reba Wells Grandrud

Albuquerque to Arizona in 1982.

While working in the mid-1980s as a research historian
for Gerald A. Doyle & Associates, a Phoenix architectural
firm known for historic preservation projects, Grandrud
became intimately familiar with John H. Slaughter's

San Bernardino Ranch in southeastern Cochise County. Although she's worn many historically-inclined hats since then, she has continued her involvement with the ranch through today.

A "Roads Scholar" (speaker) with the Arizona Humanities Council, Grandrud has held interesting positions: Chief Curator, Arizona Historical Society in Phoenix; Research Historian for Yuma Crossing Foundation; the first Heritage Fund Planner for Arizona State Historic Preservation Office (SHPO), and SHPO Historian/Coordinator of the National Register of Historic Places.

Retired from SHPO in 1998, Grandrud spent the next two years as director of the Arizona Historical Society Museum in Papago Park. She was a leader in the successful movement to resurrect the Arizona Women's Hall of Fame program in 2002. In 2003-04, Grandrud and James Garrison, Arizona State Historic Preservation Officer, formed the Inventory of Arizona Historic Cemeteries Working Group, county volunteers who are compiling, as an Arizona Centennial Legacy Project, a comprehensive inventory of every historic burial site in the state.

Today, Grandrud continues as a historical consultant and an active volunteer in leadership positions, or as a board member, for a wide range of nonprofits including Partnership for National Trails System, Anza Trail Foundation, Old Spanish Trail Association, Arizona State Committee on Trails, Arizona History Convention, Pioneers' Cemetery Association, Phoenix Corral of Westerners and Sunnyslope Historical Society – in addition to co-authoring *Addie Slaughter: The Girl Who Met Geronimo.*

About the Creator of the Curriculum Guide

The curriculum guide was written by Jean Kilker, M.A. (English), M.Ed. (Technology), NBCT (National Board Certification), who has taught language arts, reading and science.

Jean Kilker, M.A.

Currently, she is a Teacher-Librarian and former Follett Librarian of the Year. She is a member of the Public Library Advisory Board and co-chair of the State Teacher-Librarian Organization. She also teaches and writes curriculum at the university level for continuing teacher education in ESL, elementary language arts, reading and librarianship.

In addition, she has received grants and awards that benefit the students where she teaches. A native of Phoenix, Arizona, she and her husband live in Litchfield Park, Arizona, and keep in touch with their three world-traveling children.

About Five Star

Linda Radke, *President and Founder* **of Five Star Publications, Inc.**

Linda F. Radke, veteran publisher and owner of Five Star Publications, has been ahead of her game since 1985—self-publishing before it was commonplace, partnership publishing before the rest of the world even knew what |it was, and producing award-winning traditionally and nontraditionally published fiction and nonfiction for adults and children.

Five Star Publications produces premium quality books for clients and authors. Many have been recognized for excellence on local, national and international levels.

Linda also is author of *The Economical Guide to*

Self-Publishing (a 2010 Paris Book Festival first-place winner in the "How-To" category and a Writer's Digest Book Club selection, now into its second edition) and *Promote Like a Pro: Small Budget, Big Show* (a Doubleday Executive Program Book Club selection). She is a founding member of the Arizona Book Publishing Association, was named "Book Marketer of the Year" by Book Publicists of Southern California, and received numerous public relations and marketing awards from Arizona Press Women.

Five Star Publications dedicates a percentage of profits to The Mark Foster Youth Fund and other charities chosen by the authors.

For more information about Five Star Publications, the Mark Foster Youth Fund, or charities supported by Five Star authors, visit www.FiveStarPublications.com.

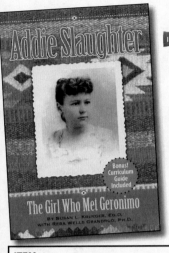

◇ Addie Slaughter
Order Form

– proves to young readers that history is NOT boring especially when retold by a child who actually lived it!

www.AddieSlaughterBook.com

ITEM	QTY	Unit Price	TOTAL
Addie Slaughter: The Girl Who Met Geronimo		$15.95	
▶▶▶▶▶▶▶▶▶▶▶▶▶▶▶▶▶ Subtotal			
* 8.8% sales tax – on all orders originating in Arizona.		*Tax	
* $8.00 or 10% of the total order – whichever is greater. Ground shipping. Allow 1 to 2 weeks for delivery.		*Shipping	
Mail form to: Five Star Publications, PO Box 6698, Chandler, AZ 85246-6698		TOTAL	

NAME:

ADDRESS:

CITY, STATE, ZIP:

DAYTIME PHONE: FAX:

EMAIL:

Method of Payment:
❑VISA ❑Master Card ❑Discover Card ❑American Express

▲ account number   ▲ expiration date

▲ signature   ▲ 3-4 digit security number

❑ Yes, please send me a Five Star Publications catalog.
❑ Send me info about the co-authors speaking at my event.
How were you referred to Five Star Publications?
❑ Friend ❑ Internet ❑ Book Show ❑ Other

P.O. Box 6698 • Chandler, AZ 85246-6698
(480) 940-8182 866-471-0777 Fax: (480) 940-8787
info@FiveStarPublications.com www.FiveStarPublications.com

NORTHVILLE DISTRICT LIBRARY

3 9082 13087 3691